Hush, Puppy

poems by

Yvette R. Murray

Finishing Line Press
Georgetown, Kentucky

Hush, Puppy

My major concern is to get my work before people; to portray my Gullah folk such as we are and such as we were and to be rich and meaningful; to be read on city buses and in subways and on planes. Art should take its place as one of the necessities of life. I write for trees and rivers and all the lies that have been told about them. I write for red rice, candy ladies, the fush man**, sweetgrass, bare feet, wrought iron gates, my enchanted urban forest, and of course . . . hush puppies . . .

Paraphrased from Charles White and injected with Gullah by me

**fush man [fush man]-Noun; fish man; man who sells fish

Copyright © 2023 by Yvette R. Murray
ISBN 979-8-88838-255-4 First Edition
All rights reserved under International and Pan-American Copyright Conventions. No part of this book may be reproduced in any manner whatsoever without written permission from the publisher, except in the case of brief quotations embodied in critical articles and reviews.

ACKNOWLEDGMENTS

"2:1 Ratio" *Weekly Hubris*
"A Geechee Death: Vallejo", *Barzakh*
"Accents", *I am a Furious Wish* Anthology
"Angles", *Fall Lines*
"Come Back; Dis Ya' Home", *I am a Furious Wish* Anthology
"Line Street", *Catfish Stew*
"Minstrel Man", *I am a Furious Wish* Anthology
"Notes from the Back Pew of Mother Emanuel AME Church" as "Homage", www.agatheringtogether.com
"Port City", Ukweli: Search for Healing Truth
"R.K.", as "Rice Kingdom", *Ukweli: Search for Healing Truth*
"Saturday Mornin' in Washington Park", *Kakalak*
"Spring Street Ghazal", *Weekly Hubris*
"Walk on Water", www.mermaidsmonthly.com

REFERENCES

The Afro-American Tradition in Decorative Arts by John Michael Vlach

Grass Roots: African Origins of an American Art by Dale Rosengarten

Row Upon Row Seagrass Baskets of the South Carolina Lowcountry by Dale Rosengarten

Publisher: Leah Huete de Maines
Editor: Christen Kincaid
Cover Art: "Shadow World" by Linda Fantuzzo
Author Photo: Yvette R. Murray
Cover Design: Elizabeth Maines McCleavy

Order online: www.finishinglinepress.com
also available on amazon.com

Author inquiries and mail orders:
Finishing Line Press
PO Box 1626
Georgetown, Kentucky 40324
USA

Table of Contents

Line Street 2
Port City 3
Notes from the Back Pew of Mother Emanuel AME Church 4
Carolina Blues 5
Easy Livin' 6
You From Downtown (part I) 7
You From Downtown (part II) 8
Saturday Mornin' in Washington Park 9
A Geechee Death 10
Stone Steps 11
Manifesto 12
Them 13
Avenger of Lost Souls 14
R. K. 15
Spring Street Ghazal 16
2: 1 Ratio 17
I Was White 18
The Lazy Susan and the China Cabinet Used to Argue 20
Inheritance 21
Angles 22
Your Music 23
Ode to the Ladies in the Front of The Room 24
Ode to the Creases in my Pants 25
Death of a Neighborhood 26
My Nostalgia Ain't Like Yours 27
Dear future African Americans 28
Self Portrait as Sweetgrass 29
Bring Back the Cornerstone 30
Church Mother Dance turns Georgia Blue 32
Minstrel Man 33
Walk on Water 34
Accents 35
Come Back; Dis Ya' Home 36

CALL

Line Street

corner stores, candy ladies, and dirt,
grandmothers with eyes all over their bodies,
a yad man *, fush man ** and Barbara, the woman who
did hair in her kitchen.

In this kingdom, lived
magnificent energies of one purpose.
Grandchildren of bondage
watering little sprouts with love,
and scolding as if the two were one.

Some with less; some with more.
Enough was always enough there.
Working men eating lunch on a stoop
cashiers struttin' to the second shift at Edward's
and the flow of Friday five o'clock laughter
over a plate of hot, fried fush *** and a cold one!

I etch stone tablets
because those at the bottom of the mountain
bask in a lovely unknown.
Hush now. I must tell it right.
Ghosts are listening
in the silence of rusty locks.

Gullah Dictionary:

* yad man [yad man]-Noun; yard man or gardener
**fush man [fush man]-Noun; fish man; man who sells fish
***fush [fush]-Noun; fish

Port City

You wear the evening hour
so very well. It hugs all the curves
and loves your cobblestone gams.
Mesmerized, I am, by the mysteries
of you. Closed red lips.
Secrets of indigo and mulatto
that ghosts tell as we stroll
all manner of metropolis found.
I am lost in the swirl
of steel, blood and glass.
Phalanges folded intimately.
Your shadow leaping back into azaleas
as if you wish not to be seen
because you do keep secrets from me:
of Coffin-Trees on avenues
and still winds that blow. Still.
My rhythm is yours and yours alone,
my love.
I will not share with the moon
for I am jealous.
Though not a god at all.
A simple man who desires
the complicated love you have to give.

Notes from Back Pew of Mother Emanuel A.M.E. Church

In the middle of any night
one hot pink Jimmy Choo stiletto lies on the floor.
Rain pours against twelfth story windows.
The soiree is over and passion complete.
A misplaced corporate girl tosses like flotsam.
Against a background of snoring
and Egyptian cotton sheets
this nightmare rages:
Her footprints as they vanish from
Palmetto-lined streets.
Spray from the Atlantic drying
on her pecan brown skin.
A flavor she can hardly recall.
Many magnolia scented seasons have gone
and the impasse hovers.
Stiff pillow of regret.
Of this she dreams:

> *Picaninny braids*
> *We used to call them*
> *Thick, knotted diadems of ancestry*
> *Lay patiently on our necks.*
> *We would run around without shirts*
> *And nobody cared.*
> *And the sun,*
> *The sun would place*
> *Bronze brushstrokes*
> *On our flat nipples.*
> *Tea parties, not in Boston,*
> *But Memphis and Charleston*
> *Were our social scene,*
> *Stickforks and mud pies.*
> *We knew just whom to invite.*
> *Fishnet stockins and hair's all pressed*
> *Black patent leather shoes clickin'.*

Carolina Blues

The South is home to
a kind of old, rusty blues
that can only come from
rings around an aged eyeball that blinks
in time with the rock
of a chair on a porch.
Grandchildren of bondage
Without their minds rub scars
Of others and rock, rock, rock.

Our puppies have deep hearts that smolder,
carry New Jack dreams.
We Carolinas
both lay claim to the sky itself!
Maybe these new blues
will be the fire
that can put out the fire
started by the 2nd Earl of Warwick in 1619.

Easy Livin'

When from brown turns bright green
and the shrill laughter of children
conjures recollections
of jewelry from four o'clocks and mudpies,
honeysuckle hunts and bare feet.
When the robins return,
sunset decides to wait for late supper.
When blue is the color of the crabs,
the dresses get shorter and curtains lighter in color.
When open is the pool but the schoolhouse is shut
comes lemonade in the sweetest shades,
barbecue sauce battles.
We will cook whole hogs,
laugh at old jokes,
catch balls gone crazy,
touchdown, home run
wipe the sauce off a seasoned chin,
dig deep for the coldest beer,
sit rocking on some porches,
sipping sunshine from real glass glasses.
When smells of freshly cut grass and
different hands clasp across a fence
fit right up on the shelf
with high school football,
treble clefs and swinging hips
then dark edges lift up a little.

You From Downtown? (part I)

>   Doosy Choosy Alley
>   The Boulevard
>   The Burn
>   The Manor

Beloved mantra of old kickball champs
Love parades of our holiday college kids.

Holidays and summers our college kids.
The tat, tat, tat of drum, drum, drumlines.

Drumlines and science, math and chemistry.
Too excellent to stay so away we flew.

How excellent we flew and did we sing!
The stride of soldier on her mother's front porch.

The stride of soldier on his mother's front porch
Backyard kickball. Graduation day.

Graduation days are our holy days
"Run to the corner store, hear baby?"

Corner stores closed/Candy ladies gone.
Beloved mantra of old kickball champs.

You From Downtown? (part II)

> The Burrough
> Westside
> Eastside
> The Drive

Grown wild like ivy in our mother's yards
We now drive our own fine, German cars.

Our fine cars down these cobblestone streets
We have grown rich and wild away from you.

Welcomed in fertile soil away from you
Corner stores closed/Candy ladies gone.

Candy ladies gone/Corner stores closed.
No scattered seeds can bloom a forest.

Not an enchanted forest can they bloom.
The new sprouts dream pretty history.

Dreams of a pretty new history future!
Who will sew up their dreams if they rip?

If they rip, the dreams, who will mend them now?
Grown wild like ivy in our mother's yards.

Saturday Mornin' in Washington Park

Clack of wrench in hands of a tall man is the same today as any other day almost Fragrant bap of a basketball that hits hits hits Small staccato laughter of children bounces against rowdy titter of oldheads clowning young bucks in barbershops Farmers' market banter Flap of white sheets on a clothesline at a Grandma's house The hum of that Grandma Left right left right left right on concrete Tick tack of wooden earrings for sale Water from a hose pushing suds down a Toyota Camry Backyard over the fence laughter Deep sizzle of fish dropped chicken dropped fries dropped Rustle of a plastic bag popped open then filled Moan of a city bus Sniffing of a dog being walked Pop pop pop in a tennis match Teeny tiny wheel aches Crack of ball meets bat Roar of a familiar crowd Clack clack of the wrench again a deep soft sigh then her hand in the small of his back Every neighborhood has Saturday lyrics

A Geechee Death: Vallejo

Why, of course, I will die in Charleston
on a cobblestone street wearing one
high heeled patent leather shoe
because it had just stopped raining
and the cobblestones were still slippery.
South Carolina, not West Virginia!
Pearl of the South.
And I shall eat boiled peanuts from a sweetgrass basket
on my way to Condon's to get me another shoe!
Where I will finally be able to stick my actual foot
into the shoe before I buy it. Imagine!
I will get caught up in a parade with the Burke High School
marching band even though I left my instrument
in my empty home on an empty shelf that is itself empty.
But my stomach will still be full from the peanuts.
A fried jumbo shrimp and a tall skinny French fry will come walking
towards me on Broad Street.
Such a lovely couple.
We will chat briefly.
They will expound upon preferring stationary bikes
to the treadmill.
Yvette R. Murray will insist on having the "R" in my name
on my tombstone because that's what I have always done.
On that afternoon it will again start raining.
This time cats and dogs. Frogs will sing
"Oh, Happy Day" because I am gone, gone, gone
though not until the sun comes out pulling
steam from the concrete.
The devil will chase his wife.
All on a Thursday.

Stone Steps
    (a bop for Linda Fantuzzo's "Shadow World")

A person can run up and down those stone steps
and still not be a person. Not to them.
Our shack the only house with stone steps
'cause my Daddy the plantation stone mason.
My mama the midwife so we seen lots
of life. Lots of death. And a life that feels like death.

Up and down the stone steps.

My Daddy claim Igbo and my Mama Maasai.
The two met in a pest house on Sullivan's Island
and a short thousand years began.
Years that begat my brother and I to bondage.
Begat to bondage and dealt for another's pleasure.
Too pretty. Too strong. Too much.
Too much for a mama-a proud Maasai mama-to bear.
So, without her mind, on a silent dark blue night she . . .

Up and down the stone steps.

The fire could be seen from the Ashley River
But river water didn't do no good. Not enough.
Never enough to put out a mama's pain.
But there were no people inside. Just property.
A distant splash was drowned out by the clamor
as the drinking gourd led us away. Far away.

Up and down the stone steps.

Note: "Shadow World" by Linda Fantuzzo is the cover art.

Manifesto

        Ring the bell.
    I ring the bell for
        Gullah Geechee dark whispers.
    I ring the bell for
        desolation after establishment.
I ring the bell for tiny fingerprints in red plantation brick
            ring, ring, ring the bell

Them

        We
never thought you had
flowed so secret and still
        We
knew you would not decipher
our genome could build
and forge steel
Blues can bring
Blues can bring
Blues can bring
        We
never thought you had
a biblical envy
a biblical envy
while we fed your young

        We
bought the land while the milk
dripped from the lips of the young
        We
did not think about the imprint
and how the rhythm would begin to beat
inside of our progeny:
a wild, uncontrollable amour
an unending nighttime if
Blues did bring
        We
held heat within minds
underneath Christian civility
a biblical envy
of our blacks.

Avenger of Lost Souls

I am greater than god Hurrican,
Holy One of the Carib.
My name is unpronounceable to you
so don't even attempt.
They give us new names
as they have always done.
But I call with Mother tongues.
Rage, rage, Sisters and Brothers of the night and day.
Call out for our lost children.
Spawned by cold clash with the Sahara
we drag the ocean from its den
cast wide bands and surge, surge,
crush all of what our children built with their hands and backs.
Now I am the end.
Awakened by cries from piles of
bones on the ocean floor
the righteous roil of my rage
begins to blow.
If my fancy be Charleston or Sanford or Louisville
I will leave no stone unthrown.
Listen, listen if you can,
bite into belief in this bitter legend.

R. K.

Eight grains of rice remain
on a gold trimmed plate
after Sunday dinner

Far away from the swamp
away from the mud
a hoe rusts on the back porch

Gravy drops dark like blood
onto a bright white tablecloth
next to pan bread crumbs

Cypress tree centerpiece
casting Gullah Geechee shadows
since 1685.

Silverware dancing slowly
in the drawers of a buffet
crammed full

with the fruit
of a Pullman Porter's
tree. Almost

every inch of the front room
wall covered
with Normal School

diplomas and degrees,
kin and faces,
awards and funeral programs.

R.K.: Rice Kingdom. Rice kingdom refers to the dominance of rice as the second major agricultural export in 18th century South Carolina. Maintenance of the Rice Kingdom depended HEAVILY on the labor of enslaved people and it made fortunes for slavers. The Rice Kingdom could not and did not thrive after the civil war ended and the freeing of enslaved peoples!

Spring Street Ghazal

On a corner-crowded avenue you'd look
Too hard and get that hood look.

Sad girl, sad, drag footfalls in daylight
She is drenched if only you could look.

Better take your time now, blue suit,
Get your cappuccino and a good look.

Dragonflies hover in a garden nearby.
Squirrels dance on hot wire. Should look.

Nests in the "E" of the word "Store"
Life carved in asphalt. Understood? Look.

A spiderweb across pecan trees
Black-hooded kid with a wood look.

Yvette squints and comes the vision:
Seeing the whole if only you would look.

2:1 Ratio

When
All the
Gullah folk
meet at the sto'
we speak about how
to cook stone ground grits right.
That 2:1 ratio.
Instant is like the biblical
abomination. That ratio
reveals itself in refined spaces too
like
cheer squads,
boardrooms. It
does not feed. Not
an exquisite dish
to share with new neighbors.
This 2:1 ratio?
It comes dragging the cruel vestige
of a past life so dark/so twisted
one can only speak of it in whispers.

I Was White
(For the Mende Song and all of its Singers)

I was white
before James Brown wrote
that song saying it so loud.
Then the Blackness sneaked in on me
like the twilight fog off of Carolina
swamp. Dizzying, that fog is.
I tried to hold onto the side
of the mahogany dining room table
that sat next to the mahogany hutch
in the twice-used room
in the lovely, lovely home
on the hill
But I could not.

That whole scene started to melt
from the heat of empty
rice plantations and cotton fields
in my mirror.
long away road,
filthy Trailways station
that filled my rearview.
Dark, mahogany faces that resemble.
I was white.
Now, humming
songs from funerals I did not attend,
I turned myself inside out.

RESPONSE

The Lazy Susan and the China Cabinet Used to Argue

Once a year not ever twice
When I was in there all day
With ammonia and Old English furniture polish
They would argue like a married couple.
Always sure of the details but forgetting the rhythm.
They would fuss about what color Martin's tie was
Or what type of shoes Medgar was wearing that day.
Each one said they had an uncle who was a Pullman porter
And a sister who taught at the school.
Rumor is that both had no siblings.

Each piece in the china cabinet had something different to say too.
Even the teeny, tiny seafood forks.
They preached fiery sermons
of Struggle and Salvation all day.
Delicate, gold rimmed pieces,
Teacups,
Dessert plates,
Champagne flutes,
Beveled highball glasses,
Butter dishes,
Heavy pieces that "they just don't make any more".
The chatter was outrageous, but
Who better to teach me?

At some point during the day
their journey of words converged
And then they outdid each other with
Tales of cotton and rice fields, strong backs,
boycotts, HBCUs, afros
jim crow, and shiny shoes.
Long after the drying was done
I could hear them talking
loud, loud, loud to make sure I would still hear.

Inheritance

Invisible ink spilled into a third
little brown-eyed girl with glasses
and outspoken teeth.
It holds her like those heavy dog bookends
I carry from house to house
to one day leave. It helps
so she can put on your strong back:
a sweater to keep out the chill.

Like vines or blood running through
The hallways of the house we lost,
Your tall spirit shines so we can
see to read books and ancient texts.
On the walls, no picture of ancestors
next to three sets of degrees,
but space for the next
little brown-eyed girl to put one.

Your thirsty mind, your devotion to devotion,
Your stiff independence wander among
many gone things that, like you, are now gone.
Except black and white photos with scalloped
edges, where your spidery handwriting carved
names, faces and events together
as the Seabrook tapestry frays/grows
connected, always connecting.

Angles

Comes the exhausted Friday evenings.
the perfect angles on a clothesline
are the main topic of conversation.
The importance of such is known
to the pair: actually the older
not the younger so much
who, in defiance, measures the
precise angles with the new math
she got in her school
equals the spaces between pieces
even uniform skirts and socks
next to pillow cases and sheets.
It is the beginning of your whole life
and the beginning must be precise.
For the entire world is watching brown girls
to see how they will bloom.
You, my brown girl, must be precise
with all your angles.
So we will start here
with this clothesline.
Sometimes the voices become angry.
for it has been a long week for both.
Now they are at the end. But
the angles must be precise before
there is any rest or any peace or
fush sandwiches and Coke can be
bought then devoured (*fish, Honey, not fush*)
and the laughter can begin.
No homework tonight.
For on this day
the five are over and the two can now begin.

Your Music

At six, seven and eight
all I knew was
busy you and busy me together.
BJ Thomas and his raindrops.
Dionne Warwick asking for directions.
One thing was true.
The sounds were yours.
Yours to sip on.
Yours to jig to.
Yours to share.
In the early, early of my
helpless mornings, you pointed
me in right directions with
uniforms that were pressed. Just so.
Homework? Check
Lotion on legs? Check
Sweater? Check
Out the door.

Now, back in that door.
I simply stand
in the silence of musty regret.
A mind shut off
from the fresh air of the present.
A mind too intense
to simply mourn.
A mind swirling from the aftertaste
of sweet, cleansing anger.
My black dress is crisp
even now pressed just so.
One thing is still true.
The sounds were yours.
Yours to sip on.
Yours to jig to.
Yours to share.
And you chose to share them
with me.

Ode to the Ladies in the Front Of the Room

It begins at the top
with a certain tilt of her chin.
The way her head never slips below
a certain angle.
How she Serengeties a room.
Her speech crisp;
tart if ever crossed.
A bright smile reserved.
Impeccable politeness for the rest.
The way she will carve a necessary
path in concrete,
stands at the ready.
It is the timbre of her drawl,
The precision,
The way she seems to glide
an inch above ground.

                                            I sit in the back,
                                        live in her shadow.
But, oh, what a bright place it is.
It is I for whom she reaches.
I that she treats like wet clay.
I that she tells the tales of her creation.
Jim Crow, y'ass ma'am survivor
to whom I bow.

Ode to the Creases in My Pants

You, meticulous detail of mine, garner admiring looks; sit with me at the head of any table. You open doors for me like a Southern gentleman. Your power never ending. You put my fear in its place and lock it there. I feel particularly powerful when the creases in my pants are so sharp they cut the palms of my hands. Mountain ridges created by heat and spray starch on my blue linen slacks. That's that casket sharp. That conquering-a-world-that don't-want-you-sharp. I get this from my Mama. Although I, in sheer defiance, rebelled like the Russian citizenry in 1917. It was actually 1975 and that teen thing told me I didn't need no creases in my pants to make it. I could raise my fist and do anything I wanted . . . Except plow through that wall in universities or bank offices trying to get mortgages if I looked liked yesterday's newspaper left on a park bench. She insisted. And like all good rebellions mine came to an end or I came to my senses. Or I went back to my future. Generations have been wired in violence, tuned for this moment right here. She was one of the first to raise her fist by plowing through walls with creases and the magnificent intelligence, talent and wit that are in our genome. Who am I to argue with that? Not me.

Death of a Neighborhood

Crumbling with decay of battle lost,
the howls of aging wolves spread like mist
across swamps from Harlem to Boston
San Francisco and Los Angeles
Nawlins, Tulsa even Baltimore.
Root of evil tramples and stomps.
It seeks other moonlight.
Even the genteel Pearl of the South
spits brimstone and blood on a blue moon.
The Pearl melted down
into a statue of itself with feet of clay
entangled by laws, skin and blindness.
No longer an enchanted urban forest
it blinked and just let the vines crawl.

My Nostalgia Ain't Like Yours

>It's wearing a brand new pair of feet,
>The old ones got worn out,
>My nostalgia has been against the law,
>Still is in several of these united states,
>My nostalgia has water added to dilute it,
>My nostalgia has been lied on, lied on, lied on,
>My nostalgia has a shot of espresso,
>My nostalgia is brick,
>My nostalgia is wool,
>My nostalgia flows like the Nile,
>My nostalgia ain't blue,
>My nostalgia lives in the inner city,
>My nostalgia lives behind God's back,
>My nostalgia is the singularity that you drool.

Dear Future African-~~Americans~~,

Like smoke from many fires,
My mind drifted often through swamp,
Cotton fields, and woods to you.
I dreamed of you:
Wearin' shoes daily,
Readin' books in school,
goin' to college,
gettin' ya Master's.
I saw you in ya fine living room,
I saw you pound a gavel,
I saw you in ya office,
I saw you in the operating room,
And I saw you in the White House.

I dreamed of all ya businesses,
you ownin' the buildings,
and all ya big ideas comin' to life.
I dreamed of you in all ya glory.

Then I waded through the maze of years
in this swamp called America.
I set fires, doused fires
And laid brick upon brick
Until I had built you a house.

Self Portrait as Sweetgrass

Ingredients of my familiarity found
in low lying water
gathered and bent into beauty
I am I.
Overharvested.
Snatched from the earth like hair
pulled in a street brawl.
Stunning on mahogany bureaus,
sometimes twisted into a flower
to put in a Baccarat vase.

We the Creations
are a balm to generations
upon generations
hoping the light will shift
from ancestors' spirits into the world.
We grow like the lotus.
I am I.

Bring Back the Cornerstone

Corner store. Chilly bear lady.
Greasy spoon. Barbershop. All specters of a glorious childhood.
But ghosts live on in the hearts of the determined.

Bring back. Bring back.

There a little black girl once learned advanced mathematics.
Pretty algorithms even taxation and percentages.
Until the math became science became her future.

Bring back. Bring back.

Deadend street football championships. Backyard kickball.
Summer suns etched love into hearts forging bonds
Stronger than the chains used against us.

Bring back. Bring back.

My own feeds my own. Nurtures the motherless child.
Softens the childless mother. All wounds are healed.
And birthed a mighty nation.

Bring back. Bring back.

From there came the foundation we were built upon
And stood upon for generations. Limitless stars rising.
Without them we are without.

Bring back. Bring back.

Segregation/Integration/Gentrification
Pressed down between the pages and tossed
Into the womb that nurtures NOT.

We mourn this loss
As every sun rises.
We.   Mourn.   This.   Loss.
But when we look inside,
we find bones of our ancestors.
Bones that bore whips and chains,
Bones that hung from trees,

Bones that marched and cried and kneeled and sat down.
The cries of "Black Lives Matter"
echo through the Valley of American states
And
like hearing Ezekiel, we rise again,
Oh, sweet again,
to build mountains and inhale purple mist.

Church Mother Dance Turns Georgia Blue

BUMP-Bump-bump; BUMP-Bump-bump; BUMP-Bump-bump;
Step-2-3; Hip-2-3; Sway-2-3; Eyes closed; Head bop

A thread runs through it:
thread is fire,
fire is ice,
ice is blood.
Down in Georgia,
a Church Mother Dance
took me by the hand.
Blood memory dripped between our fingers.
Deep within
song of the field and praise house
burned between marrow and bone.
And then   I cast my vote…

BUMP-Bump-bump; BUMP-Bump-bump; BUMP-Bump-bump;
Step-2-3; Hip-2-3; Sway-2-3; Eyes closed; Head bop!

Minstrel Man

They are used to being entertained by us.
Even old field hollers can move the moon
It's like something only we humans do:
A dark and dandy deed at twilight.

Even old field hollers can move the moon.
Then we paint in colors and faces.
A dark and dandy deed at twilight:
Walking in the dust of children's bones.

Then we paint in colors and faces
We got all that jig and that jive, see?
Walking in the dust of children's bones:
Could be bebop or ballet or both.

We got all that jig and that jive, see?
From Middle Passage to Carnegie Hall
Could be bebop or ballet or both:
brings satin and patent leather swan songs.

From Middle Passage to Carnegie Hall
It's like something only we humans do
bring satin and patent leather swan songs:
They are used to being entertained by us.

Walk on Water

Once upon a time on vacation I met a beautiful conch shell
My mind tasted conch fritters/conch salad
My mind danced with sweet carols of the Caribbean. But
it sought my ethos,
watered the rhythms within my soul
My mind then heard urgent African dialects:
beautiful Hausa, rhythmic Igbo and exquisite Yoruba
A reckoning touched my genome
The fourth generation removed is loud whispers
My mind captured all these burning words
understood all the messages:
The only way back is the way we came,
Queen Ocean, full of death, blue and deep.
Queen Ocean, full of death, blue and deep,
the only way back is the way we came
A mind must understand these messages
A mind must capture the words
Hear its own loud whispers
Within feel reckoning/hear
beautiful Hausa, rhythmic Igbo and exquisite Yoruba
Water the rhythms within its soul
Command its ethos
A mind can dance with sweet carols of the Caribbean
taste conch fritters/conch salad
when it meets a conch shell on vacation

Accents
After Denise Frohman

Sistah, my Mama has the sky in her mouth too.
She carries beautiful Hausa, rhythmic Igbo and exquisite Yoruba
All smashed into one gumbo called Gullah.
Gullah: The language of survival.
In muck of rice fields
and muck of this republic
It flows with a rhythm so deep, deep, deep
It has to be eaten,
like all good gumbo should,
with cornbread.
We know that the beauty of this creole
is living on nothing,
thriving in mist.
Governed by the moon itself,
Gullah pounds the shore
like the tide
dragging grains of sand
to build islands elsewhere.
Hidden deep within our throats,
language of rebellion,
seen in the eyes,
heard in the tilt of a chin,
My Mama brought it to me
with the pride of bare feet.
We are yet
being used
bought, sold, traded
packed, shipped, and pilfered.
Now, poachers take Gullah like ivory
and put her on their trinkets to sell.

Note: I did not have the privilege to grow up speaking Gullah. But, oh, I love it so. My manner of speaking is, though, infused with Gullah words and phrases. I hold onto them as tightly as a hand grabbing a hat on a windy day. Gullah ingeniously belongs to my ancestors. It was the soundtrack of their survival and it is mine as well. —Yvette R. Murray

Come Back; Dis Ya' Home
(A bop for 2020)

The problem, the elder shouted,
is louder the trees speak
the less you hear
and the less you hear
fewer recipes you remember.
Less you cook, more you eat dirt.

Come back; Dis ya' home

The problem, the elder whispered,
has been around since a white lion
since about the time that money
was money. Folk walked off plantations
into another white nightmare.
Integrations and red lines
away from rhythms, away from rhythms
that breathe underwater.

Come back; Dis ya' home

Let blood memory guide you
back to Purple mindscape!
Then you will not eat dirt.
Drink sassafrass/strong horse tea,
be a midwife or potter, sew sweetgrass
and build strong mountains again.

Come back; Dis ya' home

www.ingramcontent.com/pod-product-compliance
Lightning Source LLC
Chambersburg PA
CBHW022123090426
42743CB00008B/975